The Cool, Awesome, Simple Science Series

Hands-On Physics

for Elementary Grades

by

Phil Parratore

Table of Contents

Density
Light as Air

What You Will Do

Illustrate that air has mass.

Get it Together

◆ 7' of string
◆ Yardstick
◆ 2 large balloons of the same size
◆ Sharp object
◆ A ceiling

Procedure

1. Loop and tighten the string securely around the center of the yardstick.
2. Suspend the stick from the ceiling by tying it to a light fixture, ceiling fan, etc. Make sure it is balanced.
3. Blow up each balloon to the same size and knot each end. With 8"-10" of string, attach each balloon to the opposite end of the ruler.
4. Adjust the center string until the ruler is level.
5. Pop one of the balloons with the sharp object. Observe.
6. Pop the other balloon. Observe.

A Closer Look

Air does have mass. When one of the balloons broke, the air escaped, and that side of the stick had less mass than the opposite side, causing the ruler to be unbalanced. By popping the other balloon, the escaping air from that side caused the stick to once again be level and balanced.

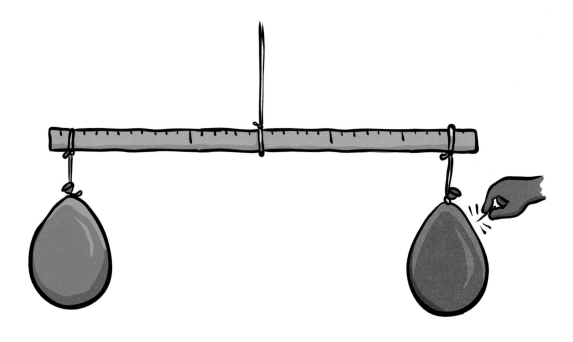

3

Squeezable Molecules

5 minutes

What You Will Do

Illustrate differences in the three states of matter.

Get it Together

- ◆ 3 plastic, resealable sandwich bags
- ◆ 50 to 100 plastic foam packing "peanut chips"
- ◆ Masking tape
- ◆ Marker

Procedure

1. With a small piece of masking tape and marker, label the 3 bags: A, B, and C.
2. Fill Bag A with 5 "chips" and seal it. This is a model of a gas.
3. Fill Bag B with 15 "chips" and seal it. This is a model of a liquid.
4. Pack Bag C tightly with the "chips" and seal it. This is a model of a solid.
5. Toss the bags in the air and observe.
6. Set the bags on a flat table, place your hand over them, and roll the "molecules."

A Closer Look

The "chips" are models, or examples, of molecules. In Bag C, a solid keeps a certain shape because its particles stay close together and do not move very fast. Bag B represents a liquid and its molecules, which are further apart than those in a solid. They move more because there is more space between them. In Bag A, the gas model, particles move around even more freely, so it is possible for a gas to fill any space it occupies.

Clean Up

Put the items in the trash when you are finished.

Density

Super Submarine

2 minutes

What You Will Do

Illustrate how different forms of the same material have different densities.

Get it Together

- ◆ Smooth square of aluminum foil (about 5" x 5")
- ◆ Bowl of water

Procedure

1. Place the foil in the bowl of water. Observe for a minute.
2. Crumple the same foil into a ball.
3. Place in the water and observe.

A Closer Look

When the flat piece of foil is placed into the water, it sinks. However, when the foil is rolled into a ball, it is filled with air pockets and it floats. This is the basic premise of how submarines work. They have large tanks that fill with air to bring them to the surface. These same tanks are filled with water and become more dense when they go under the water.

What Now?

Try this test on other crushable materials.

The Suspended Golf Ball

5 minutes+

What You Will Do

Illustrate density.

Get it Together

- Large, glass jar
- Salt
- Golf ball
- Water
- Spoon

A Closer Look

The golf ball is suspended in the middle of the jar because of the difference in densities. The salt solution is denser than the golf ball, and the golf ball is denser than the pure water.

Procedure

1. Place a golf ball in the jar and fill it halfway with water.
2. Add salt to the water and stir until the golf ball floats.
3. Allow the saltwater to stand until it is clear.
4. Slowly and carefully, fill the jar the rest of the way with pure water. Pour the water gently down the side of the glass.

Clean Up

Pour all the water down the drain.

6

Density

Which Candy Can?

2 minutes

What You Will Do

Recognize properties that affect sinking and floating.

Get it Together

- ◆ Snickers®, Milky Way®, and 3 Musketeers® fun-sized candy bars
- ◆ Bowl
- ◆ Water

Procedure

1. Make predictions about which candy bars will float and which ones will sink.
2. Unwrap each piece of candy.
3. Test your predictions by placing each candy bar in a bowl of water.

A Closer Look

Three forces of nature work together to make an object float. Buoyancy is the upward force that liquids exert against an object. Density is an object's mass divided by its volume. Displacement is the volume of water moved by a floating or sunken object.

What Now?

Try other common food items.

7

A Clean Sweep

3 minutes

What You Will Do

Display the power of a pulley.

Get it Together

- 2 brooms with handles
- 10' of rope
- 2 partners

A Closer Look

You can easily move the broom handles together even though your partners are trying to keep them apart. The brooms and rope act as a pulley system, which gives you a strong mechanical advantage.

Procedure

1. Tie the rope to the upper part of one broom handle.
2. Have each partner hold one broom.
3. Wrap the rope around both brooms three times.
4. Have your partners try to keep the broom handles apart while you pull on the loose end of the rope.

Corrugated Craziness

3 minutes

What You Will Do

Show how a large surface area can support a heavy weight.

Get it Together

- 3 sheets of construction paper
- 1 2-quart can
- 1 jar or glass
- Tape

Procedure

1. Make a crease about ¼" from the edge of one sheet of paper.
2. Using the first fold as a guide, fold a second crease back.
3. Alternate folding, back and forth, until the sheet is pleated like a fan.
4. Roll the second sheet of paper around the can and tape the ends together.
5. Remove the can.
6. Repeat Steps 4 and 5 with the third sheet of paper.
7. Line up the two circles of paper about 4"-5" from each other.
8. Place the pleated sheet on the round sheets.
9. Rest the jar on the pleated sheet.

A Closer Look

By folding the sheet of paper into pleats, you are making a larger surface area to support the jar. When the heavy jar rests on a large surface area, its weight gets distributed evenly, so it does not fall through. A flat sheet of paper, on the other hand, offers a smaller surface area that could not support the jar.

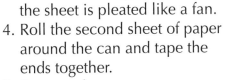

What Now?

Try making more or fewer folds on your paper to change its strength.

Force

Creepy Crawler

3 minutes

What You Will Do

Demonstrate the force of capillary action.

Get it Together

◆ Drinking straw with sealed paper wrapper
◆ Eye dropper
◆ Small dish
◆ Water

Procedure

1. Tear the top of the paper wrapper from the straw so the top of the straw can be seen.
2. Hold the bottom of the straw, then slide the top end of the wrapper down the straw until it is wrinkled and no more than 2" long. Remove the straw.
3. Put the wrinkled "crawler" on the dish, and with your eye dropper, add about 3 or 4 drops of water.

A Closer Look

When the water touched the wrinkled paper, the crawler started to grow and move. The water molecules are attracted to the walls of the paper fibers. As the water makes its way up the fibers, it is followed by more water. The force of the advancing water is enough to straighten out the wrapper.

Egg Power, Wow!

15 minutes

What You Will Do

Show the strength of a dome.

Get it Together

◆ 4 raw eggs
◆ Small pair of scissors
◆ Masking tape
◆ Several books of the same size
◆ Bowl

Procedure

1. Empty the eggs by gently breaking open the small end of each egg by tapping it on the table. Then peel away some of the eggshell and pour the egg white and yolk in the bowl.
2. Put a piece of masking tape around the middle of each shell. This will prevent the egg from cracking when you cut it.
3. Carefully cut around the eggshell, through the masking tape, so that you have four half-eggshells with even bottoms.
4. Place the eggshells on the table, open end down, in a rectangle that is just a bit smaller than one of the books.
5. Lay the books on the eggshells.
6. Keep adding books until the eggshells crack.

A Closer Look

Were you surprised at how many books you were able to place on the eggshells? Each eggshell half is a miniature dome, and domes are one of the strongest shapes. Weight on the top of a dome is carried down along the curved walls to the wide base. No single point supports the whole weight of the object.

Attention!

Use caution when working with the scissors.

11

I'm Bookin' Now

2 minutes

What You Will Do

Illustrate the strength of a cylinder.

Get it Together

- Notebook paper
- Tape
- Book

Procedure

1. Roll the paper on its short side into a cylinder. Tape it.
2. Stand the cylinder upright.
3. Place a book on top of the cylinder.

A Closer Look

The shape of a structure affects its strength. A piece of paper is not a strong material. However, when it is rolled into a cylinder it becomes stronger and the weight of the book is spread throughout the structure.

12

Magnet and Steel

1 minute

What You Will Do

Demonstrate the separation of magnetic and non-magnetic material.

Get it Together

◆ Magnet
◆ ½ cup sand
◆ Small amount of iron filings (science supply store)
◆ Plate

Procedure

1. Mix the iron filings with the sand in the plate.
2. Bring the magnet close to the plate and stir.

A Closer Look

The mixture is easily separated once the magnet is placed near the iron. The iron filings are attracted to the magnet and are lifted away from the sand.

What Now?

Repeat this activity using different powders, such as dirt, sugar, salt, etc.

Force
Rocking Candle

15 minutes

What You Will Do

Perform an amazing balancing act with two flames on a single candle.

Get it Together

- Long candle
- Round toothpicks
- 2 identical glasses

- Matches
- Knife
- Aluminum foil

Procedure

1. Prepare the candle so it may be lighted at both ends by scraping the wax off the bottom end and exposing the wick.
2. Stick round toothpicks through the candle and then balance the toothpicks between the two glasses. You may have to adjust the toothpicks a bit until the candle is semi-tilted toward the table.
3. Place your glass/candle combination in the center of the foil.
4. Light both ends of the candle and observe for a few minutes.

A Closer Look

When the candle is lit at both ends, the end tilting downward will burn more wax. This will cause it to get lighter and tilt upward. The other end, now tilting downward, will burn more wax until it becomes lighter and tilts upward. This causes the candle to begin to rock back and forth, often quite vigorously.

Attention!

Use caution when working with flames. The dripping wax is hot. Do only under adult supervision.

Clean Up

Place the foil in the trash after the melted wax has cooled.

14

Spit Wad

2 minutes

What You Will Do

Demonstrate how a difference in air pressure can move an object.

Get it Together

- 16-ounce glass soda bottle
- Small piece of paper

Procedure

1. Make a small paper spit wad.
2. Place the bottle on its side.
3. Place the spit wad into the neck of the bottle about $1/2$".
4. With your mouth level with the bottleneck, blow hard into the bottle.

A Closer Look

Instead of blowing the paper in the bottle, you blew it out of the bottle. When you blew in the bottle, you actually increased the air pressure. To balance the pressure inside and outside, the extra air inside the bottle escaped through the neck, taking the spit wad along with it.

Attention!

Do not throw the spit wad at anyone.

Supercharged Super Balls

5 minutes

What You Will Do

Illustrate the conservation of momentum.

Get it Together

- ◆ Large superball (toy store)
- ◆ Small superball

Procedure

1. Drop the large ball, waist high, to the floor. Notice how high it bounces back.
2. Do the same with the small ball.
3. Now place the small ball on top of the large ball and drop them together from the same height. Notice how high each ball bounces back.

Note: Be sure to drop the balls straight down. They will bounce at an angle. It may take a while to get the hang of this.

A Closer Look

The small ball bounced back higher than before. This is because the large ball transferred some of its energy to the small ball when the two balls collided. Because it gave away some of its energy, the large ball could not bounce back as high as before. This is an example of conservation of momentum.

Untearable Tissue

5 minutes

What You Will Do

Prove the shock-absorbing power of a large surface area.

Get it Together

- ◆ Tissue
- ◆ Cardboard tube from a roll of paper towels
- ◆ Rubber band
- ◆ Table salt
- ◆ Broomstick

A Closer Look

The tissue will not rip. The force you apply to the broomstick is not going directly to the tissue. There are many tiny spaces between the salt crystals, which absorb most of the force, and only a small fraction is applied to the tissue.

Procedure

1. Wrap the tissue around one end of the cardboard tube.
2. Secure it with a rubber band.
3. Fill the cardboard tube about halfway with table salt.
4. Hold the tube in one hand and the broomstick handle in the other.
5. Place the broomstick handle in the open end and push hard on the broomstick handle. Try to rip the tissue.

Clean Up

Put the salt and the tube in the trash.

What Now?

Have a partner hold the tube while you try to push on the broom handle.

17

Uptight Cups

3 minutes

What You Will Do

Overcome the forces of cohesion and adhesion.

Get it Together

- 2 identical heavy-duty plastic cups
- Ice water
- Hot water
- Room-temperature water

Procedure

1. Use your finger to spread a few drops of room-temperature water around the bottom of one cup.
2. Place the wet cup inside the other cup.
3. Attempt to pull the cups apart. Do not bend them.
4. Now, put ice water in the inner cup and dip the outer cup in hot water.
5. Attempt to pull the cups apart once again.

A Closer Look

At first, it was a bit difficult to pull the cups apart. When you fill the inner cup with ice water, the cup contracts. Hot water causes the outer cup to expand. This allows enough space for you to break the forces and pull the cups apart. Cohesion is a force that pulls water molecules together. Adhesion is the tendency of water molecules to stick to the cup.

Breakfast Lubricants

5 minutes

What You Will Do

Demonstrate how lubricants reduce friction.

Get it Together

- Two slices of toast (dry, and not the "ends")
- Jelly (any flavor)
- Spreading knife
- Toaster

Procedure

1. Make the toast.
2. Rub both slices of toast together. Notice the crumbs as friction wears away both pieces of the toast.
3. Thickly spread the jelly on one side of both slices of toast.
4. Again, rub the two slices of toast together.

A Closer Look

A great deal of friction was created when you rubbed the two dry pieces of toast together. Friction is a force that appears when one surface rubs against another surface. The dry toast has rough crumbs that stuck together. When jelly was spread over the toast it acted as a lubricant that reduced the force of friction.

Attention!

If you do your own toasting, be careful with the hot toaster and the knife.

Clean Up

Eat when complete.

Friction

By a Nose

1 minute

What You Will Do

Illustrate friction in an amazingly comical way.

Get it Together

- ◆ Lightweight, metal spoon
- ◆ Paper towel

Procedure

1. Use the paper towel to wipe any excess oil off your nose and facial area.
2. Breathe lightly into the inside of the curved part of the spoon.
3. Touch that part of the spoon to the tip of your nose.
4. Move the spoon around slightly and release it very slowly.
5. If you feel the spoon stick to your nose, release it completely. If it starts to slip, move it around again until you find a better sticking point.

A Closer Look

The spoon will stick to your nose. Although the metal and your nose seem smooth, they are actually slightly rough. When you slide the metal over the skin, this roughness tries to stop the sliding. Whenever roughness prevents two surfaces from sliding over each other, it creates a force called friction. It is friction that holds the spoon to your nose.

What Now?

Try your chin, cheek, forehead, etc.

Egyptian Engineering

20 minutes

What You Will Do

Show how frictional forces can be minimized.

Get it Together

- Shoebox
- 12" of string with a small rock tied to one end
- 10 straws
- Tape
- Several small rocks or heavy toys
- Table

Procedure

1. Tape the free end of the string to one end of the shoebox.
2. Place the small weights or toys in the box and place the box at the end of the table.
3. Drop the weighted string over the edge and observe.
4. Now, place the straws under the shoebox and repeat Step 3.

A Closer Look

The rollers, or straws, helped reduce the friction between the box and the table so the box started to move. Without the straws, there is too much friction, and the box will not move. The rollers make moving heavy weights possible much the same way as the ancient Egyptians used wooden rollers to move the stones needed for their pyramids.

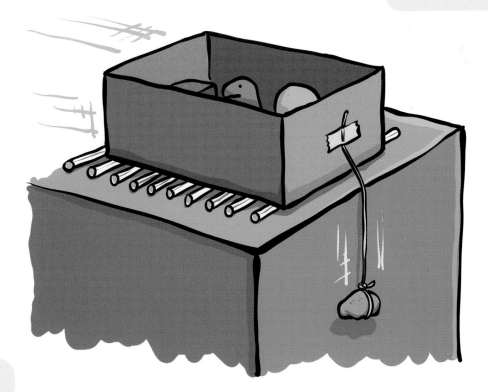

What Now?

Experiment with different amounts of weight on the string and in the box. Try different-sized rollers.

Fantastic Friction

2 minutes

What You Will Do

Compare friction among various objects.

Get it Together

- ◆ Smooth piece of wood
- ◆ Metal tray
- ◆ Various small objects: eraser, ice cube, pebble, wood block, matchbox, etc.

A Closer Look

Some objects move more easily than others because there is less friction between their smooth outer surfaces and the surface of the wood or metal. The rougher objects have more friction and move very little if at all.

Procedure

1. Arrange the selection of small objects in a line along the edge of the wood.
2. Slowly raise the wood until the objects begin to move.
3. Repeat the activity using the metal tray.

What Now?

Use different materials for the base surface, such as plastic or glass.

22

Friction is All Wet

1 minute

What You Will Do

Investigate friction in water.

Get it Together

- 2 shallow bowls
- Tennis ball
- Smooth rubber ball (i.e. racket ball)
- Water

Procedure

1. Place a ball in each bowl.
2. Attempt to spin each ball.
3. Place a small amount of water in each bowl.
4. Repeat Step 2.

A Closer Look

The water acts as a lubricant and causes the balls to spin a bit faster. The smooth surface of the rubber ball moved faster than the rough surface of the tennis ball because there is less friction on smoother surfaces.

Rub, Rub, Rub

5 minutes

What You Will Do

Demonstrate that lubricants decrease friction.

Get it Together

- ◆ Two 3" square wooden blocks
- ◆ Bar of soap
- ◆ 2 metal jar lids
- ◆ 1 tsp. cooking oil

Procedure

1. Rub the two wooden blocks together very quickly and feel the temperature.
2. Rub the bar of soap several times over the surfaces of the blocks.
3. Once again, rub the blocks together and feel the surfaces. Compare the difference in temperatures.
4. Rub the metal lids together rapidly and feel the temperature.
5. Apply the cooking oil to the lids.
6. Once again, rub the metal lids together and feel the surfaces. Compare the differences in temperature.

A Closer Look

Friction results when objects are rubbed together. Much of the energy required to make the surfaces move across each other is converted into heat. Soap and oil are lubricants used to coat the surfaces of moving objects to enable them to slide past each other more easily. Lubricants create less friction and less heat.

24

Science Friction

10 minutes

What You Will Do

Observe friction among various surfaces.

Get it Together

- 2 rulers
- Measuring tape
- Marble
- Book
- Tape

- 12" each of wax paper, crumpled sheet of aluminum foil, and sandpaper
- Long, flat surface

Procedure

1. Make an incline track by leaning the two rulers next to each other on top of the book.
2. Place the wax paper at the end of the ruler track.
3. Release the marble near the top of the track.
4. Measure the distance from the bottom of the track to the location where the marble stopped.
5. Do this several times and use the average distance.
6. Repeat Steps 3, 4, and 5 using the aluminum foil, and then the sandpaper.

A Closer Look

Friction is the force that slowed the marble and made it stop. The sandpaper had the shortest average distance because its rough surface created the most friction. The marble traveled farther over the aluminum foil and farther still over the wax paper. The more friction between an object and a surface, the quicker the object slows down.

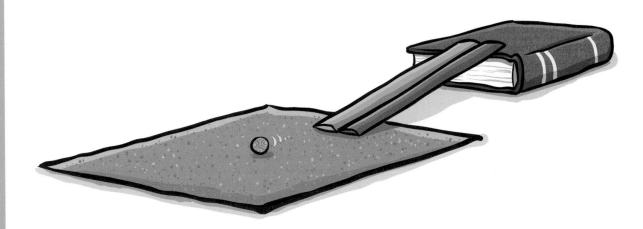

What Now?

Repeat the experiment using different materials such as cardboard, wood, glass, sheet metal, etc.

Singing Glass

2 minutes

What You Will Do

Demonstrate how friction can cause a glass to vibrate.

Get it Together

- Very thin, stemmed glass (parent-approved crystal works great)
- Vinegar
- Small, shallow bowl
- Table
- Soap and water solution

Procedure

1. Wash the glass and your hands in the soap and water.
2. Pour a small amount of vinegar in the bowl.
3. Hold the base of the glass firmly on the table.
4. Wet the index finger of your free hand with the vinegar, and gently rub it around the rim of the glass several times.

A Closer Look

The glass starts to sing when its rim is rubbed. Washing the glass and your hands removes any oil that might act as a lubricant. The vinegar dissolves any remaining oil and increases the friction between your skin and the glass. Friction allows your finger to temporarily "stick" to the glass molecules, pulling them apart to the point of tension. Then your finger slips off that point and "sticks" to glass molecules at another location. As you rub your finger around the rim of the glass, this symphony of molecular movement is turned into sound vibrations, which your ears perceive as a pitch.

Attention!

Use caution when working with fragile crystal glassware. Get permission before doing this activity.

Straining the Oil

2 minutes

What You Will Do

Determine the effect of water and oil on each other.

Get it Together

◆ Clean, metal strainer with small holes
◆ Vegetable oil
◆ Water
◆ Cup or glass
◆ Sink or bucket

Procedure

1. Pour a small amount of oil in the strainer and shake the strainer lightly to get all the holes completely coated.
2. Pour excess oil back in the container.
3. Carefully and gently pour some water into the strainer.
4. Over a sink or bucket, touch the bottom of the strainer.

A Closer Look

An invisible elastic skin from the oil keeps the water from running through the strainer. The oil fills the gaps in between the metal screen and allows for the water to be held in the strainer. This adhesion is called surface tension. The touch of your finger produced enough friction to break the surface tension between the oil and the holes in the strainer.

27

eat Moves

10 minutes

What You Will Do

Demonstrate the heat-conducting properties of different materials.

Get it Together

- Large, plastic bowl
- Metal spoon
- Plastic spoon
- Wooden spoon
- Stove
- Pot
- Water

Procedure

1. Feel the handles of the spoons. The temperatures should be the same.
2. Heat a few cups of hot water and carefully pour it into the bowl.
3. Place the spoons in the bowl and allow them to sit in the hot water for a few minutes.
4. Take the spoons out of the water.
5. Once again, feel the handles of all the spoons.

A Closer Look

The metal spoon heats up the fastest because it is a good conductor of heat. Heat conduction is the transfer of energy between objects that are in direct contact. As the temperature of the water rises, its molecules move faster until they collide with the molecules of the spoon, transferring heat. The molecules of the spoon get excited and they collide with neighboring spoon molecules until the heat is transferred all the way to the top. The plastic and wooden spoons are not good conductors of heat so they do not feel warm when you touch them.

Attention!

Have an adult heat the water on the stove.

What Now?

Try to rank the spoons from coolest to warmest. Try different types of materials. Use a bowl of ice water in place of hot water and repeat the test.

Steamboat Willie

What You Will Do

Model a steamboat.

Get it Together

- Clean sardine can
- Long, metal, hollow tube with lid (i.e. cigar container)
- Modeling clay
- Long tray of water
- 2 small, thin candles
- Ice pick
- Matches or lighter

Procedure

1. Place the candles in the sardine can.
2. Pour about 1 ounce of water in the metal tube.
3. With the ice pick, punch a small hole in the screw cap of the metal tube. Secure the lid on the tube.
4. Mold the clay around the tube and use it to attach the tube to the sardine can. Make sure the tube sits over the candles.
5. Place your boat in the water.
6. Light the candles that are under the metal tube and wait for the water to boil.

A Closer Look

As the candles heat the water in the tube, the water boils and turns to steam. The steam molecules move fast and spread out, and they escape with great force through the hole in the cap. This force pushes the boat forward, just like a steamboat.

Attention!

Use caution when using matches. The ice pick is sharp. Ask an adult to assist you.

Unburnable Cup

5 minutes

What You Will Do

Demonstrate the heat-conducting properties of water.

Get it Together

- ◆ Unwaxed paper cup
- ◆ Butane lighter
- ◆ Water

Procedure

1. Fill the cup with water.
2. Hold an open flame directly under the cup for a few minutes. Do not allow the flame to touch the cup.
3. Carefully place a finger in the water.

A Closer Look

The cup does not burn. This is because the thin paper simply transmits the heat directly to the water. The water absorbs the heat and, in turn, protects the paper.

Attention!

Use caution when working with a lighter. Do only under adult supervision.

Heat Energy
Waxy Needle

5 minutes

What You Will Do

Demonstrate that metal is a good conductor of heat.

Get it Together

- ◆ Metal knitting needle
- ◆ Pot holder
- ◆ Candle
- ◆ Matches or lighter

Procedure

1. Drip candle wax on the knitting needle making lumps at various points as the wax dries. (You may want to keep a piece of newspaper under the candle when you do this.)
2. Hold one end of the needle with the pot holder.
3. Hold the other end of the needle over the flame of the candle at a 45˚ angle.

A Closer Look

The wax seems to be "walking" on top of the needle. As the needle gets hot, its molecules move quickly and collide. This energy is conducted along the length of the needle, making it hot enough to melt the wax.

Attention!

Use caution when dripping the hot wax on the needle. Do only under adult supervision.

An Action Reaction

5 minutes

What You Will Do

Demonstrate Newton's Third Law of Motion.

Get it Together

- 2-liter soda bottle
- Rubber stopper or cork that fits the bottle
- 1 cup vinegar
- Baking soda
- 10 round pencils
- Funnel
- Flat surface

Procedure

1. On the flat surface, line up the 10 pencils next to each other about 1" apart.
2. Place about 1" of baking soda in the bottom of the bottle.
3. Use the funnel and fill the bottle with the vinegar.
4. Quickly place the cork on the bottle and lay the bottle sideways on the pencils. Make sure it is not pointing at anyone.
5. Wait for the cork to shoot out of the bottle and observe the movement of the bottle.

A Closer Look

When the baking soda and vinegar react, carbon dioxide gas is produced. As more gas forms, the pressure in the bottle increases, forcing the stopper to shoot out of the bottle. The action of the stopper shooting forward caused a rolling-backward reaction from the bottle. This is an example of Newton's Third Law of Motion which states, For every action, there is an equal and opposite reaction.

Attention!
Do not aim the bottle toward anyone.

Clean Up

Flush the baking soda/vinegar combination down the drain.

Bounce That by Me Again

1 minute

What You Will Do

Demonstrate Newton's Third Law of Motion.

Get it Together

- ◆ 12" ruler with a groove in the center
- ◆ Several marbles

Procedure

1. Place several marbles in the center of the ruler. They should touch each other.
2. Roll another marble toward the others with a sharp snap of your finger.
3. Repeat Step 2 using two marbles.

A Closer Look

The force from the single marble was transferred through the stationary marbles. When that force reached the last free marble, it shot off the end of the ruler. The force from two marbles caused the last two marbles to shoot off. This demonstrates Newton's Third Law of Motion which states, For every action, there is an equal and opposite reaction.

Come-Back Can

30 minutes

What You Will Do

Demonstrate that stored energy can convert to motion.

Get it Together

- ◆ Any size coffee can
- ◆ 2 plastic coffee can lids (that fit the coffee can)
- ◆ String
- ◆ 2 strong, long rubber bands (about ¹/₂ the length of the can)
- ◆ Can opener
- ◆ Weight, about ¹/₂ lb.
- ◆ Punch or awl
- ◆ Flat, smooth surface

A Closer Look

The can rolls on the floor in the same direction you pushed it, then it starts to return to you in the opposite direction. As the can starts to roll, the rubber bands and weight are twisting and storing the energy of the rolling motion. When the can stops, the rubber bands unwind, releasing the stored energy and sending the can back to you.

Procedure

1. Cut off both ends of the coffee can with the can opener.
2. Punch 2 holes in the middle of the two plastic lids about 1" to 1¹/₂" apart.
3. Thread a long rubber band through the holes in one lid. Repeat for the second lid.
4. Tie the ends of the rubber bands together inside the can with a piece of string.
5. Tie the weight in the center of the can so that it hangs down from the rubber bands.
6. Carefully place the lids on the can. The weight should not touch the metal in the can.
   NOTE: At this point you may need to make a few minor adjustments so everything fits just right.
7. Gently roll the can on a flat, smooth surface.

Attention!
An adult should remove the ends of the coffee can.

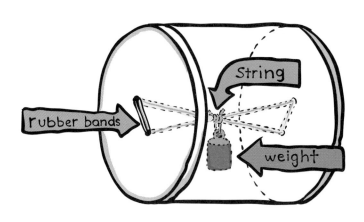

34

Crazy Coins

1 minute

What You Will Do

Demonstrate Newton's First Law of Motion.

Get it Together

◆ 5 coins (Be sure that the five stacked coins are thicker than the coin you choose to "shoot")
◆ Table

Procedure

1. Stack the five coins on a flat table.
2. Place the sixth coin about 2" from the stack.
3. With a hard flip of your finger, hit the coin into the stack.

A Closer Look

The bottom coin was resting until the coin crashed into it with a great force. The top coins stayed put because they did not receive the force. This is an example of Newton's First Law of Motion which says that an object at rest tends to stay at rest unless acted upon by an outside force. The top coins were subject to a force called inertia, or resistance to movement.

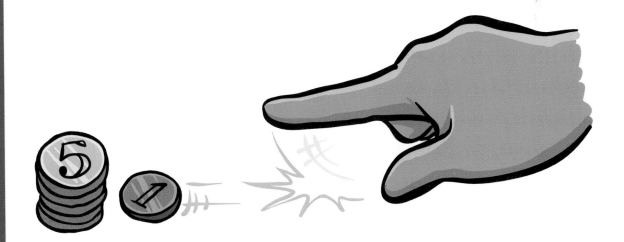

Get Into the Swing

5 minutes

What You Will Do

Demonstrate how a pendulum operates.

Get it Together

◆ Small, soft stuffed toy, such as a stuffed animal
◆ Several feet of string
◆ Ceiling hook

Procedure

1. Find a ceiling hook attached to a ceiling beam. The area around the hook should be cleared of any objects.
2. Take a piece of string long enough to tie around the ceiling hook and still reach your chest.
3. Tie the open end of the string to the soft stuffed toy.
4. Hold the toy and back up with it until you can hold it as high as your nose (but don't touch your nose).
5. Let go and stand very still. Do not move your face forward.

A Closer Look

The toy never hit your nose. When you lifted the pendulum to your nose, you had to do a little work. When you let go, all the effort you used to lift the toy went right into your pendulum. On the return swing, the pendulum could only come as high as you had lifted it before because that is when it ran out of energy. Friction with the air caused the pendulum to slow down.

Attention!

Do this experiment under adult supervision.

What Now?

Try a longer string. Give the pendulum a little shove before you start.

Ramp and Roll

2 minutes

What You Will Do

Observe the conversion of potential energy to kinetic energy.

Get it Together

◆ 2 identical long planks of wood
◆ Several thick books
◆ 2 sets each of identical balls (i.e. tennis, golf, racket, etc.)

Procedure

1. Set up the two ramps next to each other. For one ramp use only one book, and for the other ramp, use several books.
2. Roll one ball down each ramp at the same time.
3. Repeat using the other set of balls.

A Closer Look

The ball that went down the steeper ramp traveled farther. When you placed the ball at the top of the ramp, you gave it stored energy, or potential energy. Releasing the ball caused the potential energy to be converted to motion, or kinetic energy. The higher your ramp is, the more potential energy you give the ball to convert to motion. Friction slows down the ball and causes it to stop.

37

Sandy Physics

5 minutes

What You Will Do

Demonstrate momentum.

Get it Together

◆ Jar with straight sides and screw top lid
◆ Sand
◆ Long wooden board
◆ Towel
◆ Several books
◆ Water

Procedure

1. Rest one end of the board against the top of several books.
2. Place the towel at the base of the board.
3. Fill the jar with water and screw on the lid.
4. Roll the jar down the board.
5. Empty the jar and fill it with sand.
6. Roll the jar down the board.
7. Empty half of the sand out of the jar and roll it down the board.

A Closer Look

The water, like any liquid, rolled down the incline plane very easily. However, the jar of sand was a bit more difficult to roll down the board. The half-full jar actually stopped. This is know as conservation of momentum. This is similar to when one pool ball strikes another. The first pool ball stops and transfers all of its energy to the second pool ball; if the second pool ball has the same mass, it will move off with the same speed and direction. Momentum is defined as the weight of an object times its speed.

Swing Time

10 minutes

What You Will Do

Observe the transfer of kinetic energy.

Get it Together

- 6 pieces of strings that are slightly different lengths
- Hanger
- 5 metal nuts or washers
- Teaspoon

Procedure

1. Tie the metal nuts or washers to the strings.
2. Attach the teaspoon to the sixth piece of string.
3. Tie each string to the hanger keeping the spoon at the end.
4. Hold the hanger steady from the top and swing the teaspoon.

A Closer Look

The swing of the teaspoon moves along the hanger and transfers some of its energy to the metal washers, causing them all to move. Energy of motion is called kinetic energy.

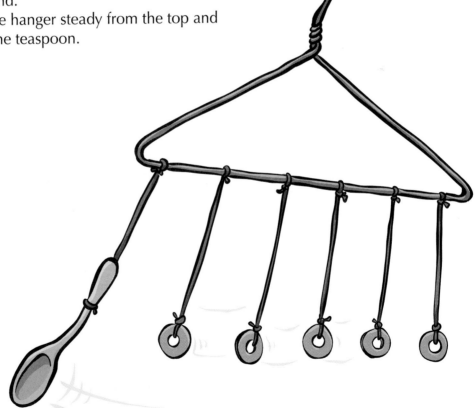

What Now?

Repeat this activity with different weights and different-sized strings.

39

Bigger is Better

5 minutes

What You Will Do

Display how a lens magnifies objects.

Get it Together

- Plastic bucket
- Clear, plastic wrap
- String or large rubber band
- Sharp utility knife
- Warm water
- Various small objects

A Closer Look

All the objects appear bigger than their original size because you have made a convex lens. Telescopes, microscopes, cameras, and eyeglasses all use the same basic principle of the convex lens.

Procedure

1. Have an adult cut a large circle on the side of the bucket.
2. Place the plastic wrap on top of the bucket. It should loosely cover the top of the bucket and hang over the rim.
3. Tie the cover tightly with string or a rubber band.
4. Slowly pour warm water into the plastic until it overflows.
5. Hold the small object(s) inside the bucket and observe from the top.

Attention!
Use caution when cutting with the sharp utility knife.

What Now?

Try other liquids in place of water.

Optics
Mirror Images

What You Will Do

Observe how mirrors show opposite reflections.

Get it Together

- ◆ 2 small mirrors
- ◆ Masking or electrical tape

Procedure

1. Place one mirror about 12" from your face. Look at your face and wink your right eye and notice which eye seems to wink.
2. Tape two mirrors together so that they open and close like a book. Open them so they form a 90° angle with each other.
3. Looking into both mirrors at once, wink at your reflection again. Notice which eye winks.

A Closer Look

You can see objects in a mirror because light reflects, or bounces, off of them. A flat mirror reverses your right side and your left side so when you first winked into one mirror with your right eye, the left eye of the reflection winks back. When you looked into both mirrors and winked, the reflection's right eye winks back. The second reflection reverses the first reversal, putting things back the way they are without mirrors and without reflection.

Attention!
Tape any sharp edges and use caution when handling the mirrors.

© Carson-Dellosa CD-7324

Optics
We're Beaming

2 minutes

What You Will Do

Illustrate how light travels in a straight path until it strikes an opaque object.

Get it Together

- Flashlight
- 5 index cards
- Binder clips or modeling clay
- Hole punch
- Table next to a wall
- Dark room

Procedure

1. Stack the index cards together and punch a hole through all five of them.
2. Stand each card upright so that the long side of the card is on the tabletop. Use binder clips or modeling clay to hold the cards upright.
3. Space the cards about 3" apart. Make sure the holes are lined up.
4. Darken the room and place the flashlight in front of the card nearest you. Observe.
5. Now move one of the cards about an inch and repeat step 4.

A Closer Look

When the cards are perfectly aligned, the light from the flashlight is visible on the wall. When you moved one of the cards out of alignment, the light was not visible. Moving the card changed the direction of the path of light, proving that light travels in a straight path or line until it strikes an opaque object.

42

Who Turned Off the Lights?

1 minute

What You Will Do

Illustrate how polarized filters block light.

Get it Together

- ◆ 2 pairs of polarized sunglasses
- ◆ Any small object

Procedure

1. Hold one set of sunglasses in one hand and the second set in the other hand.
2. Above the small object, place one of the sunglass lenses on top of a second sunglass lens, making sure they are aligned in the same direction.
3. Look at the small object.
4. Now rotate the top lens 90°.
5. Look again at the small object.

A Closer Look

When two polarized lenses are combined at a 90° angle, no light can come through. This is because light can only come through tiny horizontal or vertical slits in the filter. When the slits of the two lenses are aligned, light can still get through. When the lenses are at a 90° angle, the light that gets through one filter gets blocked by the second filter so you can no longer see the object.

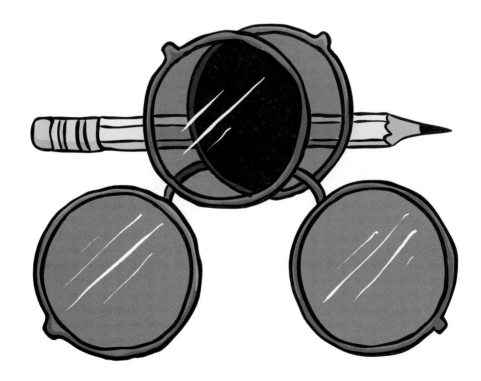

An Uplifting Experience

1 minute

What You Will Do

Demonstrate the force of a partial vacuum.

Get it Together

- Small latex balloon
- Drinking glass
- Water

Procedure

1. Fill the glass halfway with water.
2. Place the balloon in the glass and blow it up.
3. Lift the glass by the neck of the expanded balloon.

A Closer Look

The friction of the balloon against the glass is sufficient to prevent the balloon from easily pulling out. When this friction is great enough, the balloon will not pull out easily because air cannot get into the bottom of the glass. As you pull on the balloon, the air pressure in the glass is lowered, allowing you to lift the glass with the balloon still attached. The balloon sealed off the glass so air could not get in. In order to remove the balloon, the space it occupies must be replaced by air, but since air cannot get in, the balloon cannot get out.

Hungry Pickle Jar

10 minutes

What You Will Do

Demonstrate how heat affects the strength of air pressure.

Get it Together

- Wide-mouthed pickle jar
- Round balloon
- Matches
- Sheet of paper to burn
- Drinking straw
- Water

Procedure

1. Fill the balloon with water until it is a bit larger than the opening of the mouth of the jar.
2. Roll the paper and place it halfway into the jar.
3. Light the paper on fire and drop it completely into the jar.
4. Quickly place the balloon on top of the jar. Observe.
5. Try to remove the balloon from the jar without breaking it. It cannot be done.
6. To remove the balloon, push a straw halfway into the jar.
7. Grasp the tip of the balloon and gently pull it out.

A Closer Look

The balloon is sucked into the jar because the flames ate up most of the oxygen and formed a partial vacuum. With the lack of air in the jar, the water balloon took the place of the missing air. The balloon cannot be removed from the jar until you balance the pressure between the inside and the outside by letting air in. The straw allows this to happen.

Attention!

Do this activity only under adult supervision. Use caution when working with matches and burning paper.

Get a Grip on It

2 minutes

What You Will Do

Demonstrate vacuum formation.

Get it Together

◆ Clear, plastic, drinking glass
◆ Plastic sandwich bag
◆ Several rubber bands

Procedure

1. Place your hand inside the bag.
2. Push the bag down into the glass, leaving the top to fold over the rim of the glass.
3. Use the rubber bands to very tightly secure the bag top around the rim.
4. Reach into the glass and pull the bottom of the bag out of the glass.

A Closer Look

The bag is difficult to pull up because a partial vacuum was formed underneath it. When you sealed the bag to the jar, you trapped a certain volume of air inside the jar. In order to remove the bag, the space it occupies must be replaced by air, but since air cannot get in, the vacuum prevents the bag from getting out.

Race Day

5 minutes

What You Will Do

Display how the speed of different car designs is affected by air resistance.

Get it Together

- ◆ 2 identical toy cars
- ◆ Thin cardboard
- ◆ Tape
- ◆ A partner
- ◆ Scissors
- ◆ Hair dryer
- ◆ Wooden board

A Closer Look

The curved-top car is more aerodynamic and will resist the force of the dryer easier than the box-type car. The air passes over the curved top easier and faster than the box-type car with the flat front because the flat front encounters greater air resistance. Note the design of most cars today. They have a curved shape either in the front, back, or both.

Procedure

1. Cut a strip of cardboard as wide as the car, but long enough so that you can shape it across the length of the car in a curved, semi-circular pattern.
2. Tape each end onto one of the cars.
3. On the second car, tape another piece of cardboard that is shaped in a boxy, rectangular-looking top, like a trailer truck.
4. Place the wooden ramp at an incline.
5. Place the cars at the top of the board. Have your partner hold the cars in place.
6. Turn on the hair dryer and place it at the base of the board. The dryer should be blowing up the incline.
7. Release the cars.

Sip It!

1 minute

What You Will Do

Illustrate vacuum formation.

Get it Together

- Plastic drinking straw
- Needle or pin
- Your favorite beverage

Procedure

1. Take the needle or pin and stick it through the straw in many different places near the top.
2. Place the straw in your beverage and try to drink it. The holes should be above the drink level.

A Closer Look

When you inhale on a straw, you create a vacuum by lowering the air pressure on the part of the drink that is in the straw. The greater pressure on the surface of the liquid outside of the straw forces the drink up in your mouth. When there are holes in the straw, the pressure cannot be reduced because air comes in through the holes. With no pressure difference to force the drink up the straw, the drink stays put and does not reach your mouth.

Attention!

Use caution when placing the pin through the straw.

The Last Straw

1 minute

What You Will Do

Demonstrate the strength of air.

Get it Together

◆ Fresh, raw potato
◆ 2 drinking straws

Procedure

1. Place the potato on a flat surface.
2. Take one straw, leaving the top open, and raise it above the potato.
3. Quickly, with force, try to stick the end of the straw into the potato.
4. Hold your thumb over the top of the second straw.
5. Repeat Step 3.

A Closer Look

The straw bends when you do not hold the top closed with your thumb. The closed straw cuts into the potato. Air is made up of invisible gases, which have pressure. The trapped air inside the second straw makes the straw strong enough to cut into the potato. The push of air inside the straw keeps it from bending.

Up with the Cup

1 minute

What You Will Do

Show that air pressure can lift objects.

Get it Together

◆ 2 3-ounce paper cups
◆ Scissors

Procedure

1. Place one cup inside the other.
2. Hold the cups about 2" from your mouth and blow very hard between the rims of the cups.
3. Now cut off the bottom of one of the cups.
4. Place the other cup inside this one.
5. Repeat Step 2.

A Closer Look

When you blow between the rims of the cups, you force air between the cup bottoms. As the air pocket expands, the top cup pops out. However, the same thing happens when you cut the bottom out of the cup. This happens due to the shape of the cups. Because the sides are tapered, the air that moves down the sides between the cups has a squeezing effect, which forces the inner cup to move upward from the bottom.

Attention!

Use caution when working with scissors.

50

You Big Bag of Wind

5 minutes

What You Will Do

Demonstrate the Bernoulli Principle.

Get it Together

- ◆ 10-gallon garbage bag
- ◆ Watch

Procedure

1. Squeeze the air from the bag.
2. Blow up the bag and time how long this takes.
3. Squeeze the air from the bag again.
4. Hold the open end of the bag about 10" from your mouth.
5. Using only one large breath, blow as hard as you can into the bag.

A Closer Look

The bag inflates much faster the second time. When you blow a stream of air into the bag from a distance, you decrease the air pressure inside the bag. Higher pressure from the outside atmosphere causes air to rush into the bag to balance out the difference in pressure. This is an example of the Bernoulli Principle.

Attention!

If you become short of breath, stop at once.

51

Are You Listening?

5 minutes

What You Will Do

Demonstrate how sound travels.

Get it Together

- ◆ 2 plastic foam cups
- ◆ 3 yards of string
- ◆ Pencil
- ◆ Toothpick
- ◆ A partner

A Closer Look

The sound of your partner's voice travels from the cup through the string to your cup. Your partner's voice causes the string to vibrate. Vibration of the string carries the sound. When the string is pinched the vibration is cut off and no sound is carried.

Procedure

1. Use the pencil to poke a small hole in the bottom of each cup.
2. Break the toothpick in half.
3. Put the ends of the string through the holes. (Use the pencil to help push it through.)
4. Tie the ends of the string to the middle of each toothpick.
5. Give one cup to a partner.
6. Move apart until the string is straight and very tight.
7. Have your partner talk gently into the cup while you listen.
8. Gently pinch the string while your partner is still talking.

What Now?

Try the same experiment again using yarn, fishing line, or thread to see which carries the best sound.

Bottled Music

5 minutes

What You Will Do

Demonstrate that vibrating air columns are perceived as pitch.

Get it Together

- ◆ 6 small-mouthed bottles or tall glasses
- ◆ Metal spoon
- ◆ Water

Procedure

1. Pour different amounts of water in each bottle.
2. Line up the bottles from least full to most full.
3. Gently tap each bottle with the metal spoon.

A Closer Look

The bottle with the most water has the highest pitch. The number of times the object vibrates (moves back and forth) is called frequency. As the frequency increases, the pitch of the sound gets higher. Tapping the bottles causes the air in the bottles to vibrate. The shorter column of air above the water vibrates faster, and produces a higher pitch. As the height of the air column increases, the pitch of the sound gets lower.

Good Vibrations

2 minutes

What You Will Do

Depict how vibration speed affects pitch.

Get it Together

◆ 12" plastic ruler
◆ Flat desk or table top

Procedure

1. Place the ruler on the desk so that 3" are sticking off the desk.
2. Place the palm of one hand over the part of the ruler that remains on top of the desk.
3. Using your free hand, pluck the end of the ruler that is hanging over the desk. Notice the sound of the pitch and the frequency of the vibrations.
4. Now slide the ruler off the desk to the 4" mark and repeat Step 3.
5. Continue this until you get to the end of the ruler.

A Closer Look

You changed the pitch as you changed the distance of the ruler. When the piece of ruler that hangs over the desk is short, it vibrates the surrounding air at a higher frequency and the pitch is high. As the ruler gets longer, it vibrates at a lower frequency and the pitch is lowered.

Attention!
Do not allow the ruler to flip out of your hands.

TOING!

Hear Ye, Hear Ye

2 minutes

What You Will Do

Show that sound waves travel differently through different materials.

Get it Together

- Plastic sandwich bag
- Pencil with eraser
- Wood block
- Water
- A partner

A Closer Look

Sound travels better though the wood than through the air. Sound travels through solid objects faster because the particles are closer together than those in liquids or gases.

Procedure

1. Fill the bag with air by blowing into it. Seal it.
2. Hold the bag next to your ear.
3. Cover your other ear with your other hand.
4. Have your partner tap the bag lightly with the pencil eraser.
5. Now fill the same bag with water and repeat Steps 2, 3, and 4.
6. Hold the block next to your ear and have your partner tap the block lightly with the eraser.

What Now?

Use different common objects.

Moving the Sound

1 minute

What You Will Do

Model how sound waves are transmitted.

Get it Together

- ◆ 6 identical coins
- ◆ Flat surface

Procedure

1. Place five coins in a straight row on a flat surface with the edges touching each other.
2. Place the sixth coin an inch away from one end of the row.
3. Place four fingers of one hand on the first four touching coins (one finger on each coin). Hold them firmly in place.
4. With your other hand, and using your fingers, snap the free coin against the end of the row and notice what happens to the last coin. You may feel a slight vibration in your fingers when you snap the coin. You may need to try this several times until you get the hang of it.

A Closer Look

The last coin bounced away from the other coins. The coin first struck is vibrated and this vibration is transmitted through the other coins until it arrives at the last coin, which is free to move. Sound vibrations travel through air in much the same way. Sound waves are transmitted from air particle to air particle until they reach your ears.

Sound
Music, Music Everywhere

2 minutes

What You Will Do

Show the relationship between frequency and pitch.

Get it Together

◆ Square cake pan
◆ Rubber bands of different widths

Procedure

1. Place the rubber bands around the cake pan.
2. Pluck the different rubber bands. Observe the vibrations and listen to the pitch.

A Closer Look

The length, width, and placement of the rubber bands determine the type of sound produced. The thicker the rubber band, the lower the sound because they vibrate slower. The thinner rubber bands vibrate faster, causing a higher sound.

What Now?

Use different-sized containers to see if it changes the sound.

Seeing Sound

30 minutes+

What You Will Do

Demonstrate how sound waves cause vibration.

Get it Together

- Balloon
- Scissors
- Clean soup can
- Can opener
- Rubber bands
- Tape
- Glue
- Mirror about ¹/₂" square
- Flashlight
- Wall

Procedure

1. Use the can opener to remove both ends of the soup can.
2. Cut the neck off of the balloon and stretch the remaining part tightly over one end of the can.
3. Hold the balloon in place with the rubber bands and tape the edge of the balloon to the can to keep it from slipping.
4. Glue the mirror (face out) to the stretched balloon, about a third of the way in from the edge of the can.
5. Now shine the flashlight onto the mirror at an angle so that a bright spot from the mirror can be seen reflected on the wall.
6. Hold the can very still (or set it on a table, braced so it won't roll) and sing or shout into the open end of the can. Observe the spot of light on the wall.

A Closer Look

The reflected light moved because of the vibrations from the sound of your voice. The noise you made traveled through the air, like ripples in water, until it reached the balloon. The balloon absorbed the sound waves and transmitted them to the mirror causing it, and the reflected light, to move.

Attention!

Have an adult assist you with the can opener.

58

Sound the Alarm

4 minutes

What You Will Do

Illustrate the Doppler effect.

Get it Together

- 6' of strong string
- Alarm clock with a bell or a watch with an alarm
- A partner

Procedure

1. Tie one end of the string very securely to the clock or watch.
2. Set the alarm to go off in a few moments.
3. Have your partner stand about 8'-10' away from you.
4. When the alarm sounds, carefully start twirling the clock or watch over your head. As it twirls, let more string out until you are holding the string near the end.
5. Compare what you hear and what your partner hears.

A Closer Look

The alarm sound travels in waves through the air and spreads out in all directions. When you are twirling the alarm it sounds the same to your ears. However, your partner hears a changing pitch. The pitch sounds higher when the alarm comes closer to your partner because the sound waves are bunched together and more sound waves hit her ear each second. Further away the sound waves are more spread out and the pitch is lower. The change in sound wave frequency is known as the Doppler effect.

Attention!
Do this activity in an open area.

Sounds Good to Me

3 minutes

What You Will Do

Observe transmission of sound waves through the air.

Get it Together

- ◆ Large, round cookie tin
- ◆ Sheet of plastic wrap
- ◆ Strong rubber band (to fit around the tin)
- ◆ Wooden spoon
- ◆ Granulated sugar
- ◆ Baking tray or other metal pan

Procedure

1. Stretch the plastic over the cookie tin to make a drum.
2. Stretch the rubber band around the tin to hold the plastic taut.
3. Sprinkle the sugar on top of the "drum skin."
4. Hold the baking tray very close to your drum and tap it hard with the wooden spoon. Observe.

A Closer Look

The sugar will dance up and down on your drum. When you hit the tray, the metal and the air around it vibrate for a fraction of a second. These vibrations in the air are called sound waves. They quickly work their way through the air to the "drum skin" causing it to vibrate so that the sugar moves.

60

Spoon Bell

5 minutes

What You Will Do

Demonstrate how the pitch of sound can be changed.

Get it Together

- Metal spoon
- 30" of string
- Table

Procedure

1. Tie the handle of the spoon to the center of the string.
2. Wrap the ends of the string around your index fingers.
3. Place the tip of an index finger in each ear.
4. Lean over so that the spoon hangs freely and tap the spoon against the side of a table. Listen carefully.
5. Shorten the string by wrapping more of it around your fingers.
6. Repeat Step 4.

A Closer Look

You heard a sound like a church bell. The vibrating molecules in the spoon hit against the string's molecules, and the energy is transferred up the string to your ears. When the vibrations travel across a long string they spread out and have a lower frequency and a lower pitch. When you shorten the strings the movements are more compressed, resulting in a higher frequency and a higher pitch.

Strauss with Straws

5 minutes

What You Will Do

Demonstrate changing pitch with changing lengths of air columns.

Get it Together

◆ 8 drinking straws about ¹/₄" in diameter
◆ Scissors
◆ Tape
◆ Table

A Closer Look

The longer straws produce a long frequency wave, or low pitch, while the shorter straws produce a short frequency wave, or high pitch.

Procedure

1. Place an 8"-10" strip of tape, sticky-side up, on the table.
2. Cut all the straws to different lengths (about ¹/₂" difference for each one).
3. Place the straws, from shortest to longest, on the tape, each separated by about ¹/₂".
4. Place another piece of tape on top of the straws, sticky-side down, touching the tape between the straws.
5. Blow across the tops of the straws to produce sounds with varying pitch.

What Now?

Attempt to play a simple tune, like *Mary Had A Little Lamb.*

The Tell-Tale Watch

1 minute

What You Will Do

Demonstrate how sound waves travel.

Get it Together

- 30" paper tube
- Ticking watch or clock
- A partner

Procedure

1. Place the watch in an upright position.
2. Have your partner hold a watch in front of one end of the tube.
3. Place the other end of the tube next to your ear.

A Closer Look

Sound waves normally spread out in circles from the sound source while getting weaker as the circles get larger. The tube confines some of the sound waves so that they cannot spread out. Therefore, the sound waves travel along the inside of the tube without diminishing very much.

TICK TICK TICK

Sound
Wave Bye-Bye

1 minute

What You Will Do

Model the movement of sound waves.

Get it Together

◆ Spring toy
◆ A partner

Procedure

1. While standing still, have your partner hold each end of the toy and stretch it out about arm's length.
2. Gather some of the coils from one end, and gently push them toward the other end. This will bunch up some of the coils at that end.
3. With your partner standing still, let go of the gathered portion and allow it to move toward the other stationary end.
4. Repeat several times.

A Closer Look

A sound wave is a series of compressions and expansions. The compressions are the tightly coiled sections where the molecules are crowded together. The expansions are the spread-apart sections of the toy where the molecules are fewer and farther apart.

Attention!

Do not let go of the spring toy when it is stretched. It could snap back and cause injury.